D1522365

Sweet Solitude

Sweet Solitude

NEW AND SELECTED POEMS

Leonard A. Slade Jr.

excelsior editions

State University of New York Press
Albany, New York

Published by State University of New York Press, Albany

© 2010 State University of New York

All rights reserved

Printed in the United States of America

No part of this book may be used or reproduced in any manner
whatsoever without written permission. No part of this book may
be stored in a retrieval system or transmitted in any form or by any
means including electronic, electrostatic, magnetic tape, mechanical,
photocopying, recording, or otherwise without the prior permission
in writing of the publisher.

Excelsior Editions is an imprint of State University of New York Press

For information, contact
State University of New York Press, Albany, NY
www.sunypress.edu

Production by Kelli W. LeRoux
Marketing by Fran Keneston

Library of Congress Cataloging-in-Publication Data
Slade, Leonard A.
  Sweet solitude : new and selected poems / Leonard A. Slade Jr.—
Excelsior editions.
    p. cm.
  ISBN 978-1-4384-3345-5 (hardcover : alk. paper)
  I. Title.
  PS3569.L235S94 2010
  811'.54—dc22
                                              2009053978

10 9 8 7 6 5 4 3 2 1

For Roberta Hall Slade and Minitria Elisabeth Slade

CONTENTS

From *The Whipping Song* (1993)

From *For the Love of Freedom* (2000)

From *Vintage* (1995)

From *Pure Light* (1996)

From *Jazz After Dinner* (2007)

New Poems (2008)

There is commonly sufficient space about us. I have my own sun and moon and stars, and a little world all to myself. There can be no very black melancholy to him who lives in the midst of Nature and has his senses still.

—Henry David Thoreau, "Solitude," *Walden*

From
*Another Black Voice:
A Different Drummer*
(1988)

The Black Man Speaks of Rivers, Part 2:
A Tribute to Langston Hughes

'I've known rivers':
'I've known rivers' current 'as the world.'

'My soul grows deep like the rivers.'

I listened to Stokely Carmichael
    When furious fire heated cool air.
I shook hands with Martin Luther King, Jr.,
    Before garbage cans in Memphis.
I heard shots in Dallas
    when John F. Kennedy waved at me.

'I've known rivers.'

I heard the drums of stomachs in New York
    when welfare queens paraded the streets.
I danced to the melody of Diana Ross
    when Leontyne Price sang at the Met.
I read Sunday school lessons at home
    when Alice Walker wrote *The Color Purple*.

'I've known rivers.'

I bathed the body of a Rolls Royce
    when shacks cuddled me with love.
I plowed through books at Morehouse College
    when white men perused works at Harvard.
I moved into the mainstream
    a century after Huck and Jim journeyed down the
    Mississippi.

'My soul grows deep like the rivers.'

Acquaintances

I meet an acquaintance
whose greeting is icy.
Good evening. I am this,
I am that.
And how about you? *Courtship*
I am me.
My desire to explore her heart and soul *Curiosity, love, passion*
through Antarctica is boundless.
The ice melts. *precipitation*
There is no past.
Here we are,
discovering each other's worlds.
Another continent comes between us: *America vs Africa*
my mahogany skin, her ivory face, *Biracial love*
my woolly hair, her lips of wine
create barriers between us as we go.

Noiseless and impatient, we move to darker
regions of the soul. *(despair, anger of the reign inequality brings)*

Words. Now she has them. She wants more.

3

The Black Madonna

(for Elizabeth Langford Slade)

picking cotton on
a cold day blisters
decorated her black fingers
in the fields

She crawled on her knees
until the sun bowed
to her. Eight children
planted beneath the stars
The earth felt good to her. ~ *Regardless of how*
hard the labor, her
children made it worth
while.

You can see her now
a parched face and folded hands
Church   she kneels in a different place
drinking blood and eating bread
at the altar

Comforted white gloves feel good to her
waving to touch the sky
hymns fill the air
They feel good to her
they feel good to her

4

The Anniversary

At church
she'd bow to guest preachers
listening
to their hellfire sermons
her wig resting like graveyard grass
the preacher her half sat near her
in tails like a statue
in a cemetery.

And celebrating his anniversary
he'd dream of silver watching it
rovingly, rovingly
as members dropped it in plates
on Jesus' table.
His heart wild with greed
his money, his church, his anniversary
these belonged to others as well.

Special seats establishing his hierarchy
he'd listen for hours
to hoarse voices singing
to praises from peasants
exalting him and her.

Grinning in the light
and quiet
he'd preach next Sunday
the powerful word
the Bible
tight in his fist.

The Country Preacher's Folk Prayer

Eternal God,
We come this mornin'
with bowed heads and humble hearts.

Uh hum.

We thank you for sparing us another day
by letting your angels watch over our
bedside while we slumbered and slept.

Uh hum.

We come to you without any form or fashion:
just as we are without one plea.

Uh hum.

You blessed us when we didn't deserve it.
When we traveled down the road of sin,
you snatched us, and made us taste of the
blood of Thy Lamb.

Yes, Lord!

This mornin', touch every human heart.
Transform tears into Heavenly showers
for the salvation of sinful souls.

Yassir.

Remember the sick, the afflicted,
the heavy laden.

Open the windows of thy Heavenly home.
Let perpetual light shine in the midnight hour.

Yes, Lord!

When we have done all that we can do down here,
take us into Thy kingdom, where the sun never sets,
where there's no more bigotry, hypocrisy, backbiting;
no more weeping and wailing, before Thy throne, where
you will wipe away our tears; where we can see our
mothers;

Ma Ma!

Where, in that city, where the streets are paved in gold and
adorned with every jewel,
where we can see Jesus, sitting on the throne
of glory.

Ummmm mmmmmm a hummmmmmm.

When we get home, when we get home,
when we get home,

we'll rest in Thy bosom
and praise you forever.

Amen

God's Gender

I have heard
about God's gender
in tabernacles pontificating
Father, Son, Holy Ghost
and in schools
intellectualizing
Deism, Theism, Pantheism
and in homes nurturing
Faith, Hope, and Love.

My definition of this
Male, Female, Nurturing Creator
transcends gender
AND IS GOOD!

The Mansion

It rests between the sky and soil,
Like a sandwich
Hot in a black oven;
Arrays of suits adorn chairs
Under the stars, August Moon,
At home on a hill.

Teeth sparkle from Gleem.
And dentures dance laughter.
Governor Mary glides to a hush.
And eyes inspect.
A Bavarian folk band plays for bards
And beauty.
We clap our hands to anthems,
Hee-haws,
And accents.
Another culture melts us here.

An aide plants herself next to me
To peep at scribbled notes
Kept secret.
Moments dictate
Poetry now.
Melodies reach clouds,
Touch airplanes and stars, while
Pine trees listen in green attire.
Blackbirds eavesdrop and peek, too.

Lost among seas of white masks,
Three black faces stare,
Their hearts pulsating tunes,
Absorbed by hot air, for 90 minutes.

By the Side of the Road

They wait for all to enter,
100 small rooms,
for moms and dads,
lovers and all.
They are welcomed here.

Neon lights and a gift shop
lure them.
Two beds or one, a choice
become trampolines
for deferred sleep, dreams.
Playboy channels their movements
or Christian Broadcasting saves
King James' book an opening.

Lovers rendezvous here
searching and swallowing sweet juice
fire water, Coke,
and more.
Voices echo ecstasy
they do not hear.

Clothed or nude
wrinkled or smooth
bodies rest here:
one room, home, where
dreams differ by the side
of the road.

Race

They grin at blackness
I am brown sugar
High yellow is revered.

Do they know
my brown flesh still burns
like charcoal from their whips
and chains?
Their hungry dogs' saliva
foamed to garble strewn
meat, to taste hot blood,
running like cold water.

They call it history now.
Where are their griefs
to match my pain?
South African whites do not know.
They do not know.

Yet they smile.

Elegy for Therman B. O'Daniel

I remember his voice, rich and golden;
And his urbane manner, majestic as a king;
And how, once meeting, a smile leaped for us,
And he thundered beliefs about journals and words
And how they last.
We sang, too, his melodies
And dreamed,
Our leafs turning to poems and stories;
Our songs tremble their criticism now.

He kindled an eternal flame
That burns hearts, young and old,
And sacrificed twilight years for stars,
And enjoyed the sunrise and sunsets.

If only we could assure him now
That his work reaped harvests for all seasons,
The fruit of his labors save the world.

From
The Beauty of Blackness
(1989)

The Beauty of Blackness

The beauty of
my people

is permeating
the world

crossing races
and sexes

in South Africa
and the USA

an amalgamation
and cultural assimilation

pregnant where
regions enjoy

sophisticated language
and precision

and love transcending
boundaries and color

North and South
East and West civil

politics changed
maturing Barack Obama

and Bishop Tutus . . .

Like timber
burning blackness

we stand
like poplars

learning ourselves
and growing stately

from blood
spilled and

wounds healed
from a bitter past

made strong
by evil vomited

and cleansed
from racists' bellies

we feed the
universe whole

a oneness
of purpose

from diversity
of beings

beauty . . .

respected
for naturalness

giving birth
to love

we exemplars
of the universe

cry.

Transition

When I was eighteen
it was my urge
I must have outlets
Seasoned now
I look back
worshipping youth
of the 1960s:
two breasts fed me
kindness amidst Revolution
guns exploded, hot,
a body gone wrong
we thought
kissing death
youth craves parts, all,
old age, reverie, completeness,
ripe fruit from gardens
plucked.

Now at forty-five
my desire
courts spirits
plants seeds
removing grass
to penetrate deepness
to fill emptiness:
three fed me
Eve, Helen, Jerusalem
an apple
inward war
flying doves
sustain
transcend aching elements,
a totality:

dust, wind, ashes
King, Kennedy, Malcolm
disciples larger than life
led me.

Sleepless Now

There is a season
of arrayed lights
burning cedars

indoors. The fireplace
cuts cold,
glows

in dolls' eyes,
closed until 4 a.m.

"Mommy, Mommy, Mommy!
Santa's
been here!"

sleepless now
the
Christmas Season.

Cat

Among animals
and humans
I love the cat black
in a lap
on a cold
day
lying
still
eyes closed
to a crackling fire
and golden flames
free.

When I Heard from the Tax Man

When I read the auditor's letter,
I squirmed at an invitation to be his guest,
After I had spent a $6,000 tax refund,
How soon I became ill,
Until the audit was over,
I piled three boxes of evidence on his desk,
In a plush office tower suite,
Examining tons of receipts he concluded,
That Uncle Sam owed me an additional $2,000 refund.
I thanked him for his modern math,
Praised his judgment and meticulosity,
and kissed his invitation goodbye.

A Child's Play

There is a backyard
surrounded
with fences

of different sorts
in a city
on a hill

where a girl
jumps
rope and

inhales air
for a song
circling herself

she hops
on blades
of grass

dying in her
steps; she
ascends her height

the sky
her limit
for joy

A Black Man's Song

security is remembering
a breast nursing babes
where nipples provide
a pipeline

warm milk sucked and
a mother's eyes sparkling
like stars, understanding
blackness

babes stare and
bite a love
into rebelliousness
and forgiveness

closer now
for the joy and pain
two give all, take all
for love.

Spring

The rites of spring
bring balmy weather

a wet earth
fertile and

pregnant with
red roses and tulips

spring fever
contagious

cool now
real.

To an Apostle of Peace

We notice, Dr. King,
that America celebrates
your birthday now
a national holiday
in most states.

We observe
that your words
are louder,
your deeds nobler
since your fall
on a balcony in Memphis.

We understand
your fire
burning now
in hearts and
why your family
cried for justice.

We failed you
in Memphis, but you
gave us peace
hope and truth and
left a legacy
for children, the
oppressed

for presidents and kings.
We study your pictures
your speeches in books
your biographies
in libraries,
We feel your spirit,

You Live!

From
I Fly Like a Bird
(1992)

Birds

Seven days, each night
Red, blue, and black birds
Land on our front porch,
Hunting seeds by their feeder,
    As if at home.

Awed a million times, the birds
Whistle first; then the melody of their voices!
Singing at dawn and eventide,
They pause and spy for security,
    As if freedom were elusive.

Their presence is observed daily,
When neighbors open curtains,
To praise their congregation,
To savor a serenade in the air,
    As if yearning for communion.

Is it rare to have birds,
Acquaintances, suspicious of motives,
Seek trust and safety here—
to eat, sing, and touch humanity,
    As if time were to die?

Black Woman

Strong woman, black woman
clothed in love, exuding beauty!
I share your darkness, — *oppression or just pigment?*
     the sun in your eyes,
The brilliance of your mind,
     the lyric in your mouth,
the roots of your soul
And discover myself. *Origin / identity*

Creativity, talent

His Professor

His hair silk
from rich years
his teachings,
quiet words, I observed:

his slow walk, his
humped shoulders and
head bowed;
his breath, short

The books grasped
as if gold
under his arms
resting on yellow notes

published articles,
poems, rhythm;
performing symbols
pupils learn

his labors and
whispers
almost
gone.

Overcharged

Overcharged motel, I would not pay,
The beautiful blonde had been okay

Until she charged four nights, not three
And argued unjustly more money against me.

My high blood pressure admittedly rose
As my high voice lost control

For her refusing to admit a wrong
Provoking me to be her super Kahn.

She declined to listed to dramatic oration
And to respect my logic and explanation.

Furious now, I asked the manager
Who for some reason was the motel janitor

To review my bills for accuracy and all
And to take my number for a telephone call.

Overcharging me, a University Professor
Taking on this a dangerous oppressor.

Again my blood pressure unfortunately rose
As the manager like ice almost froze.

She couldn't understand me a mean black
Standing up to defend a simple fact.

Justice and freedom I do need
In this land known for greed.

Sometimes I wish I were President
To avoid dealing with devilment.

Drinking

is a sobering experience
like sipping vodka in a
topless bar
    multiplying movements
    till flesh burns.

Like one body becoming two
as problems diminish
    or destroy.

It is beer and wine
that build fire
for stomachs and fools
    like a wife and child
    scolding for prevention

because alcohol retains
    false power to conquer
    with empty words. It

is like the lion
    drinking blood
    from animals' guts

it is guzzling constantly:
sipping and quenching.

Its wetness is tears;
    camouflaging scars,
    breaking the heart.

[Handwritten annotations:]
- juxtaposition
- → sin, giving in to temptation.
- Vision distorted
- → Depressant
- Drinking problems away. Depressant. Further hurting yourself.

It's drowning hopes
    confusion visiting; it's
    drunken sleep and scattered

dreams transforming the now.

↳ Puzzle pieces of life became
  a reality = a mess.

And Want No More

To see her in bed
is to know
    the meaning of pain.

It's to understand a surgeon's
scalpel and why.
    How I wish,

desiring her luscious breast, its
nipple now gone with cancerous
    tissue, my kissing it before, teaching

me. Beauty is something deeper
that she is a person
    that loves tests.

How I loved the breast that
nurtured my child,
    its milk dripped on pillows

I have sinned,
worshipping selfish needs,

a honey-brown breast, now
soaking in blood,
    is like testicles removed.

How humble I am,
one breast left
    giving us more love, the same

To see a wife's breast disfigured,
cancerous cells gone
   is to know wellness

and its shared meaning
is to prolong life
   and want no more.

Garden Party

Saturday my wife
and I
strolled the Garden Party

a fountain separated two black
groups stately
sitting and observing

subjects like us
queer for daring
to melt ice.

We greeted our hostess,
caked in red grins,
and sat to "hello's"

and "so good to see you's"
then wine provoked
love and hatred,

our eyes sparkled
to clichés and rock,
we danced attached

separating our bodies
from the party, we
hugged the night,

afraid of ourselves
hungry for each other's
garden, not

to be entered here.

What Are You, Life?

What are you, Life,

with your heart
beating your
mobile body

why do you want
me
when you give
breath and gold

to kings and queens
presidents and prime ministers
making their motion
on air and ground . . .
light

why do you reserve
space in
the universe
for me

a room
a spot
for me?

Grief

A feeling you must reject
    when love is buried,
tears moistening the earth, and all

flowers droop in winter
    that promise spring
but keep you waiting.

And it's funeral chimes
    touching the heart with
blood cold and music gone.

1 April 1989

We Mourn a Sweet Soul

The strength of your years
Leaves our blood warm,
Your gentle spirit lives
In the marrow of our bones.
Stars court the moon
to glimpse at your soul:
Sweet and victorious
Celebrating life
In all the Heavens.

23 March 1989

From
The Whipping Song
(1993)

The Whipping Song

The Cardinal at my window
sings blood in my veins.
I will tell anyone who asks,
it's made my heart leap, for
who can resist songs at morning?
His clothes burn the Celestial
sun. His quickness arouses
dull senses. If I stare in
his eyes, I am his slave, yielding
to his beauty, whipped by his song.

Peace Will Come

when families plant seeds of love
and neighbors destroy walls
and nations heal wounds
from wars past;
when races bury guns and bombs
and assassinate prejudice and hatred
and when children kindle eternal flames
bearing a torch
burning a love
needed now.

For My Forefathers

For my forefathers
Whipped from Africa
Where children cried
But ships sailed on
And plantation owners were animals
Their roars echoing three-hundred years.

For my forefathers
Whose fingers pierced cotton bolls
Beneath the sun roasting human flesh
And darkness told master
To rape black women
For labor and profit.

For my forefathers
Whose masters cursed the North
And justified the South
And debated Lincoln vs. Douglass
And cited slaves in the Bible
And returned to Africa for more.
For my forefathers
Who couldn't read or write
But heard freedom ringing
After Lincoln's Emancipation Proclamation
That taught me to watch
And pray for a new day.

For my forefathers
Who loved me.

The Street Man

In New York City I saw a ragged man limp
Around Rockefeller Plaza.
I sat admiring red roses.
He hunted soda cans and crumbs
In trash barrels to feed garbage bags.
Curious,
I watched him depart,
The American Flag waving.

Love Should Grow, Not Wither

Love should be silent and whisper
As the gentle wind

Kisses
Cracked cheeks in dead winter,

Fast as the rolling thunder
Lighting the sky before stars dream—

Love should be earthy
As the laughter of children.

Love should build words in time
As the sun rises,

Leaving, as the sun sets
Rays to bloom roses,

Leaving, as the sun hides behind the mountain
Darkness that somehow yields to light—

Love should build words in time
As birds sing and fly.

Love should be free to—
Well.

For all the pain
A heart endures and a salty tear.

For love
The aching sounds and sweet breaths of life—

Love should grow,
Not wither.

Rain

The rain kisses
a cold tin roof.

It tinkles making
music and magic
as mother and child
alone hug the night.

A Plea for Peace

Let the hawk roost near
the dove
and their eyes
be mirrors, bright and shining, slow
to shut, quick to trust,
sleepless.
—lifting olive branches to travel
the sky and the land.
Silent (No message
but peace) Fly!

Before the Death of Dad

Before maggots suck your marble eyes,
before bones yield to a hollow earth, inviting
black meat to heat cold blood,

I will tell you of the dark days of youth,
of the tears soaking white pillows, of your
hollers inflicting severe pain. I still

love you, the eldest child from your fruitful
penis, your lost sheep destined to lead; I
touch you in your white casket, when I,

nearly 40, still hunger for your laughter
and ache for honeyed words. Open your eyes
in church, hear the voice of your son:

"Plant me again in my mother's womb."

Winds of Change

Cool us, sea—
hold our warm bodies,
splash your cold spit
in our faces,
sail our ship
beyond the bounds
of human thought,
guide us through winds of change.

From
For the Love of Freedom
(2000)

For the Love of Freedom

Read your dark history
Bleeding Black people;
Study your enemies' past
All about their white hoods;
Rip these pages from textbooks;
Burn them in enemies' hearts;
Replace them with the love of freedom.

The Black Hair

I have just combed woolly hair,
    Nappy and black,
    Refusing to cooperate,
    Resisting stiff grease,
    Kinky,
    Sensitive,
    Curly.
Why, beautiful hair, are you defiant?
And why are you not free?

Why Are You Laughing?

why are you laughing

with your big mouth
with your uncontrolled hysteria

why do you laugh
at Eddie Murphy movies

are you aware that
Abe Lincoln
was assassinated

and John Kennedy
and Martin Luther King, Jr.,
and Malcolm X

why do you laugh
with people in tears
then holler in bed
as you explode
with love?

The Saint

After he had taken drugs
And fornicated with a thousand women,
He decided that getting drunk would
Be perfect after shacking up one more time.
He was free until a revelation.
Now he recites chapters and verses in the Bible
Telling us to repent of our sins.
I tell him that I want to sin
One more time before becoming holy:
He puts my soul in the hands of the Lord.
I am satisfied.

A Song for the Black Woman

Let the sun rise
early in the morning
and the silence
be of love, sweet and holy, precious
and pure, quick
for new language

—through words to describe
your body and mind.
Write. (No sentiment
but for light) Create!
Darkness is my answer that makes
love tonight.

From
Vintage
(1995)

There Will Be Blacks in Heaven

There will be blacks to teach
what others don't know.

There will be Cleopatra who will
smile as she removes her crown for sleep
on a moving cloud.

There will be Haile Selassie whose
beard will be combed by angels
adoring him.

There will be William Wells Brown who will be
revising his novel, *Clotel*, for the making
of a movie among the stars.

There will be Harriet Tubman chatting
with Abe Lincoln about the condition
of blacks back home in 1993, defining
their oppression, injustice, and mental slavery.

There will be Booker T. Washington debating
W.E.B. Du Bois on the progress of blacks
and the value of integration and segregation
in the South during the good old days.

There will be Mary McLeod Bethune advising
Franklin Delano Roosevelt to speak to Bill Clinton
about the value of historically black colleges.

There will be Martin Luther King, Jr., in front
of Malcolm X, shouting to throngs,
"Free at last!
Free at last!
Thank God Almighty,
Free at last!"

Strangers

We mingled with liquid
fermented grapes.
(Bacchus praised us!)
Bread was our body.
We laughed.
Our words spread
like gardens,
water, fresh.
They nurtured growth
between strangers,
black and white.

That made the difference. → salvation

Mathew 24:14

The words of Jesus + the work of his disiples?

From
Pure Light
(1996)

Pure Light

In the evening were the glowing
moon and shining stars, a gift
moving the world. Brighter
now, rays of light,
glimmer of hope; unborn child
on a donkey sleeping in darkness.
We were falling in
Eden, Virgin Mother.
We were waiting on edge
for a new world, for centuries:
praying for you to give birth to
new love and pure light.

Calling All Black Men

Calling all Black men
Real
Responsible
Rich in love.

All Black men
(Eligible) — single
for
Black women

To love   7
and
Hold   Eternal adoration
Forever. _| exchange vows

Calling all Black men
Come on
Home Now! — stay w/ your race?

        ⤷ stop the lolly gaging and
          became what it is you're
          supposed to be...

Words

Be careful what you say.
When you use words, it
    is hard to take them back,
They pierce heavy hearts, aching hearts; they
    kill friends quickly; they don't care—
Be careful what you say.

15 March 1996

Your Life Is Over for You If

you smoke ten packs of cigarettes daily
guzzle Jack Daniels to sleep as a ritual
sit at your oak desk fifteen hours daily
take (always) the elevator instead of walking (briskly)
marry a fussbudget who worships materialism
have children that you do not want
eat fat hogs and quarts of ice cream for breakfast
destroy bridges instead of building them in relationships
hate instead of loving with all your heart.

Sunrise

How orange the sky is this morning
with sunlight breaking cotton clouds.

Fog by the river is ghostlike
and so is the hoot of the owl.

Birds sing in tall birches,
cocks crow in the barnyard.

Gum eyes open slowly—one peek
and a new day is born.

In Praise of Shoeshines

We suffered shining shoes for 300 years.
Then, one day, this bootery up North had a bargain:

> buy your shoes,
> get free shoeshines for life.

Chocolate brother bought beautiful brown shoes
from a cold vanilla sister on Saturday.

Now, he returns often for shoeshines on Sunday
and the sister rolls her bad blue eyes

forgetting history.

So Happy

Sister Rosetta rejoices.
—but we glide back
in our church seats.
What hair.
What a voice.

That's just Sister Rosetta
jumping toward Heaven
every Sunday, stomping
her feet
waving her hands

calling His name
clinching her fists
hollering and singing
about her love
for Jesus.

(Her wig landing in my lap.)

It's all right.
It's all right.
It's all right.

Innocence in Black and White

Sitting alone in my row at the Cathedral,
I kneel for prayer.
After the sermon and preparation for communion,
I begin my slow walk to the altar.
A five-year-old white child then glides
down the aisle to join me.
I smile and let her cross my path
to kneel with me.
Dropping her *Book of Common Prayer*, she smiles
at me over her perceived faux pas.
Assisting her with the right page
of another Book, I read with her
the same words, symbols with meanings
that transcend the now and contradict history.
She follows me to the altar to kneel
for the same blood
indifferent to my Blackness.
After partaking of the Supper,
she follows me to my seat
satisfied that a communion of two bodies
has elevated two souls
for all the world to see.

Budget Cuts

On the streets, in
hospitals
destitute
they're there—poor
as beggars, ashamed
as misers but visible
more and more—
asking the politicians
Why?
You can see their eyes
absorbing pain now
closing
and morticians
bringing caskets
for rest.

I Fly Away

Sometimes
after church service,
I talk to white folk
My Black suit is so dapper,
My wide straw hat
fights the hot sun
while I sip lemonade
and laugh
with blacks and whites
savoring social intercourse
under a Maple tree.
I am cool, cool, so cool.
Then Miss Manners points
to my "fly" in public,
asking,
"What's that you've got there?"
Half my shirt rests outside my pants.
I quickly pull my shirt
inside the proper place.
Laughter from the crowd
accompanies my embarrassment.
Miss Manners is secure now,
having bruised an ego,
evoked laughter, and
tasted power.
She turns red with her smile
and walks away
with her other half.
I strut in the opposite direction,
black and beautiful and proud
of what she did not know.

How Great You Are

You made the cradle of the earth.
You made the clouds for the Heavens.
You made the high hills
and the low valleys.
You assigned the moon for the seasons.
You gave knowledge to the sun.
You made darkness into light.
You laid the foundation of the world.
You gave us Africa and Asia,
North America and South America.
You shared the entire universe.
You caused grass to grow.
You brought food out of the earth.
You traveled the mighty oceans.
You stilled the raging seas.
You dwell in all generations.
You are clothed with honor
and wrapped with majesty and rich in love.
You are our everlasting God.

From
Neglecting the Flowers
(1997)

Black and Beautiful

I am African-American,
Poet of my people,
Black and beautiful,
Sweeter than chocolate candy
Lover of my queen,
Father of my child,
Conscious of my heritage,
Feet tired and hurting,
Heart heavy and hungry,
Attacked because I'm African,
Rejected because I'm Black,
Despised because I'm proud.
But I smile.
I am Black.
I am beautiful.
I am bad.
Just look at me.

Rapping My Way Home from an English Conference at Hunter College on March 22, 1997

Coming from Albany on a rocky train
Made me want to do a special thang.
I arrived at Hunter tired and mean
But the conference today made me clean.
Books and lectures and a million dollar smile
Taught me to stop for just a little while.
Thinking and rapping and hungry for a song
I deduced after meeting that I am the bomb.
Thank you, Hunter, for your mad skills,
You're the best; let's make a deal.
Come to Albany and you will learn
One love from me it'll be my turn.

Chill out!
Peace out!
You're my heart!

Reverend Hotair

You preached that people
Should treat others the way
They want to be treated.
You hooped and hollered
Until balls of sweat
Popped from your forehead.

You ran up and down the aisle
Raising your hand to Heaven
And fell on your knees
Preaching the Word. Ahaa!

Then one night in a motel
Deacon Goodwin's wife
Gave you a horseback ride
And you rode too fast.

To preach the Word
Is to live the Word
Before dying.

Neglecting the Flowers

I work until
midnight, checking
students' papers,
kissing the moon
until cocks crow.

I write in corners
where silence
speaks loudly
and words drip
honey,

sweetening the
days filled with
sorrow. They say
I labor too hard,
teaching and writing,

neglecting the
flowers
struggling
for growth
at home.

Like Douglass

Like Frederick Douglass, I battle you,
stir your conscience, America,
so rich, with welfare and homelessness,
and crime galore, so much slavery now.

Like Douglass, I share biting truth, but
you open my heart, hoping for change, although
I smile at you through wrinkles of blood—you,
my sweet home, stir me to tears.

Bury Yourself Now

I will teach you, my students,
how to suck life's marrow
for you have ancestors sleeping
in graves—
unless you want failure
you learn our history now.

Study! For God's sake read books—
all of them—and stretch your minds!
Let learning be worshipped
and not taken for granted.
No excuses please—
(especially grandma died.
I have to work two jobs.
The bus was late).

You realize that ten million slaves
were not free to read or write.
For Heaven's sake!
        Go now!
Bury yourself
        in the
                library.

On the Death of Mothers

We shall not all meet them robed in Heaven,
Nor see ourselves with crowns of glory;
If anything, in the heat of the night,
Coming with pitchforks and sharp horns,
He will steal unsaved souls.
Come, Light, let us curse the darkness.

Tongue

In the mouth behind
sparkling with teeth
it's there—resting
comfortably like a snake,
announcer of war,
despiser of peace,
proponent of truth,
lover of lies,
character assassin,
gossipmonger,
it's there
communicating power.

Burp

you burp in public
like a bull groaning

the air polluted
by your release

To Mephistopheles

Sometimes I feel like I will explode
Just lose my religion
Till one Sunday morning
I'll kneel in prayer and sing my song
And shout when the preacher calls
　　His Name
And look to Heaven
And hope that my personal God
Will just knock the living hell out of me.

Come, Prince of Peace

Come, O Prince of Peace.
Hope needs Your eternal love.
Feed hungry hearts, heavy hearts.
Keep ajar the door of salvation.
Guide us from the darkness to light.
Hold us in Your everlasting arms.

Good Manners

I don't know why my blood boils
When I greet people who don't
Know how to speak to me.
This evening I asked a pretty woman,
"How are you?" She kept
Walking with her lips sealed
And her nose pointing toward the sky.
I was not gleeful when a yellow bird
Had to use the bathroom, not knowing
She was below. Now she knows the
Meaning of "nose out of joint."

Love

Love,
Hug me tight
So that I shall not fall
From grace.

Hatred follows me
Everywhere.
I can't travel
Alone.

Accompany me on my
Journeys.
Never leave
Me.

Love,
Hug me tight.
Keep me always
In your heart.

From
Lilacs in Spring
(1998)

I Came, I Saw, I Dreamed
(for Abraham Lincoln)

I see a child being born to save a country.
I see a spiritual giant being patient
    with a Southern belle.
I see a father grieving over the death of his child.
I hear cries and see tears showering the soul
    of a Nation.
I see parents sending their sons
    to fight for freedom.
I hear slaves praying and singing in the cotton fields.
I observe a U.S. President loved and hated,
    decisive and brave.
I see a country's savior, healing a people
    divided by war, slain by an assassin's bullet.
I see a country strong and powerful, beautiful and blessed.
I dream a better world.

The Country Club in the Academy

They were special:
Research scholars,
Published writers,
Politically correct professors.
They were elitist:
Ivy-League trained,
Holders of doctorates,
Intellectual snobs.
No way but the White way.
They were . . . now, now!
They are
Dead.

Lilacs in Spring

He sucked a thumb in Kentucky,
where his father chopped wood
for warm evenings
in December. He wore old
clothes and walked barefoot
among lilacs in spring. And everywhere
he moved, Indiana and Illinois,
laughter filled the air

as young boys teased his height
and demeaned his clothes. No
child ever praised him,
and he for his suffering honored
her, all children thought small
of his future, except her
who read her Bible and loved him
as no other person could.

He studied by candlelight,
savoring words and defining dreams
for America. He was hungry for truth
and debated the pros and cons
of slavery. He promised a united country
but blood would taint freedom.
Brother against brother
sister against sister

blacks against whites
Northerners against Southerners—
they all fought for their cause.
Our father of freedom
bathed America with hope
and then was bathed himself
in cold blood.
Children cried.

Song for a Beautiful Lady
(for my wife)

Train rides and summer thoughts
weave a tune of joy and pleasure.

How often in life
can one witness such immense wealth
and Heavenly beauty?

Boss Hogg

He enjoyed telling his members what to do
At church and in the community.
He loved being in charge, the head honcho,
Even when he was invited to family gatherings
He always found excuses for not coming.
He forgot all about the event, he said,
But the truth be known he wanted to
Emasculate my father, his deacon, publicly,
Control him, his mind and manner.
But independent thinkers cannot be slaves
And can make preachers miserable souls.
My father's convictions and values
Are rooted in *The Bible*.
No preacher can rule him.
Now I pray that my father and his preacher
Will not one day fight in Heaven.
God's angels will be reserving ringside seats.

Thank You, Abe!

Abraham Lincoln set me free,
Gave me dignity for the world to see.
Some have said he did not care
About my Blackness and the slavery affair.
But I sincerely and honestly believe
This man was called to help us breathe
Truth, righteousness, justice, and all.
America now stands proud and tall.
Thank you, Abe, for what you have done
For giving us victory that's almost won.

From
Elisabeth and Other Poems
(1999)

The Good Queen Bess
(for Queen Elizabeth I of England)

Crown—
richly colorful
like halos on rainbows,
Posture—
erectly majestic,
moving among subjects charmed.
And remembered by
Edmund Spenser with *The
Faerie Queen* and
William Shakespeare's
plays celebrating
Her mind—
brilliantly visionary
changing the world forever.

Mother Africa

We hear drumbeats
Of growth and love
In a world torn by strife,
Too big to feed our starving children.
Hands reach out and eyes weep;
We study our Continent
And greet rivers and land,
Lakes and mountains;
We dance to music
Songs praising our ancestors
Who gave us space
and our heritage
Robbed from us by oppressors.
We hear drums
Beating for freedom,
Beating for love,
Beating for us
To come home.

Working on the Farm in 1947

On the farm he learned
at five-years-old the mule's
obedience to pull while
he took short steps to
hold the plow steady
and follow.
It was the post-war years
for the world but his father
had land which needed
breaking.

Black people were farming
everywhere in the South
where cotton was king.
Even in the woods, their land,
they dynamited stumps clearing
the way for planting.
In winter weather he skipped school
to pick cotton from sharp bolls—
trembled with cold, a sign of
weakness he was told.

December 24th was Santa Claus time
in their white house on a hill,
nine children in bed warmed their
bodies, hearts beating with fear.
When morning came one bicycle and
one doll baby hugged the Christmas
tree waiting to surprise everyone.

He the eldest rode the bicycle first
down the hill from home was told,
"Don't ride too far. It's dangerous!"
So he rode slowly down the path
and lost control riding himself into
the cotton patch
Falling.

Up again he rode back home the hill
hard to climb.
Falling again. Cotton fields watched
and waited.

The sun went down.
Morning. Cotton acres greeted him.
Another day of cotton picking.
Another day to dream of school.
The doll baby cried.

Marry This Poem

marriage

If you love each other,
You will marry this poem,
Hug its spiritual ideas,
Kiss its gentle words,
Respect its body and feelings.
If you love each other,
You will be sensitive to this poem.
Adjust to its hardships and meanings,
Share its joys with red roses,
Laugh and cry, but don't forget to try.
If you love each other,
You will savor this poem.
Cherish the simple pleasures of life,
Enjoy the sunrise and sunset,
Walk passionately in the rain,
Work hard but don't forget to play.
If you love this poem, get lost in the
depths of each other's heart.
Remember, a good poem is forever.

- complex
- not always clear
-

Departure

The moon bleeds
and will not see me
in darkness.

It is possible
to love a brother
in cold blood
and still notice
how his frozen tears
can disturb the soul.

Embden Pond

As I sat on a pier
Silently kissing a mirror pond,
Waves hushed a banked stillness.
Beyond acres of water
Sailed a two-passenger boat
Through dark tree shadows
Roaring toward the mountain
Leaving behind a world, so new.

Robert Lewis (Our Samoyed)

Ghost-like with red devil eyes,
He moves like lightning
Through dancing trees
Breaking deep darkness
Daring the rolling thunder to
Beat him home.

From
Jazz After Dinner
(2007)

Jazz After Dinner

On a snowy evening I shall feel his sounds,
Quietly moaning, inviting cold air to listen,
Call pleasure from golden keys. Old friends
Will kiss their company, sit to relax and dream.
And music, crying like an elderly man
That sometimes after sunrise greets the morning
Will pervade the world, profusely fill
That evening and me, celebrating life.

And When I Die

I want a clean black suit,
A white shirt adorned with
A red necktie and cuff links,
A clean pair of black socks to
Keep my feet warm with shiny
Black shoes serving as my mirror
As I lie stretched out in this
Satin casket being confident about
My good-looking appearance
And still demanding that I get respect.
I want the family to cry their eyeballs out
With my enemies shouting with guilt
Until their wigs get lost going to Heaven.
I want the whole church to holler:
"Please don't go! Please don't go!
Boo-hoo! Boo-hoo!
Please don't go!
Please don't go!"

I Am a Black Man

I am a Black man
my history written with blood
some sweet songs of sorrow
are composed for my soul
and I
can be seen plowing in the fields
Can be heard
humming
in the night

I saw my grandfather coming to America
and I reached back in time
to help him settle in North Carolina
Leaving England forever

and heard his children cry
for freedom with his last
dime . . . he

gave his African queen twelve seeds
of promise planted deep before
slavery ended . . . and I

promised him honor and freedom
I am a Black man
proud as a Lombardy poplar
stronger than granddaddy's roots
defying place
and time
and history
      crucified
           alive
                immortal
Look
      at me and be
healed

Black Philosophy

An old field
with pearls priceless
copied for centuries
writ revisionism,

Has kept man strong
rooted in hi(story)
called common sense
culled correctly.

Gems of thought
and the love of wisdom
make man precious
make man free

Morning After Morning

This is after darkness leaves,
It is when birds sing happily,

When the cool breeze kisses clouds
And the morning rain makes love to earth.

All are asleep still,
The cat tiptoes around the house.

There is silence here again,
Morning after morning.

It happens repeatedly,
This celebration of peace,

This reaffirmation of love.

Forgiveness

Memories linger, beautiful as the moon,
Beautiful that his lying did not destroy my soul,
   and repeatedly, this terrible world;
For my adversary's son is dead, a boy young and divine,
I look at him in his white casket—I turn around
Bend down and hug lightly his father
   with my shoulder catching his tears,
His crying aloud begging God for salvation.

New Poems
(2008)

Heifer

She laughed with thunder
In her voice like a snake
Rattling and crawling to release venom
For bone and blood,
Sucking the marrow out of life.
She loved big butt cows
And with a body like an elephant
Called people names:
Heifer
Witch
Bastard
Then changed her tone
With words dripping honey.
Suddenly her asinine behavior
Began again with anyone
Who disagreed with her,
Challenged her ideas,
Complimented her sincerely.
She loved and hated,
She shouted until her foot broke.
She ceased laughing and began crying
Over past suffering and work conditions,
Inflicting pain on others
Who had helped save her soul.

Picnic

Crisp winds, radiant sunlight, the day
of happiness—maybe these are
the signs to believe the future. At least now
there are moments to laugh
before the picnic ends,
when conversation becomes
food for the soul.

More and more you learn to celebrate
the small things in life.
You know that God is watching
every day you live
giving freedom for love
peace and joy.
You may as well be God-like
at picnics, too, where
Divine light shines
and the devil runs for cover.

22 July 2007
Colonie, New York

What I Need Is

What I need is
Enough love

To last forever
What I need is

My wife
Sharing unconditional love

And my daughter
Believing in my immortality

And my mother promising
Never to forget me

In her prayers
And my friends

Accepting me for
What I am

My idiosyncrasies
My down-to-earthiness

My strengths
And my weaknesses

My country ways
And my worst days

I dream
Here and now.

I Want to Live While You Love Me

I want to live while you love me,
    While you send me cards from afar,
While telephones ring endlessly for me
    And yellow roses reach my door.

I want to live while you love me,
    And bury the past pain,
And shower tears on our souls,
    To heal before I am dead.

I want to live while you love me,
    To understand my cross
Till blood ceases to drop
    And deeper love to communicate.

I want to live while you love me,
    And never, never apologize
For what we could have done
    But celebrate the now and what will be.

Highway to Love

I want to send you
a love poem as long
as the highway
after evening
when we drive
around its dangerous
curves and climb it
slowly with you
next to me
every light and bump
in its way
enjoyed
every sound
so melodious
with radio music
we hear
we must stop
hug each other
we must kiss
each other
and remove fog
on the windows
have our hearts
slow down we must
hold each other.

I Do Love You

Everything you've given me, sparkling eyes
looking at the tears of the years, to give me
strength, massages on my back to unload burdens,
and the honey words of some saints, sacred from
hymnals, poems, and the Bible, and what
have you received in return for your oneness
with me?

The daughter from your womb. The hell of my
foolish ways. Lack of common sense. The
betrayal of hypocritical friends you warned.

I do love you. Who is to define. I love you, your
soft music, your letters stored in my heart for immortality.

I do love you.

Brothers

The hard days of youth at home
Were fraught with field work,
Preparing us for the real world.

We plowed behind mules,
Picked cotton from sunrise
To sunset,

Occasionally pausing to
Dream of another world
And crawling with humility.

We remember the cold,
The blood dripping from fingers,
The smell of dinner soon.

Weigh the cotton bags first.
Mother picked more than all,
Still strong for the family

With our looking in awe.
We remember the prayer.
Sitting at the dinner table

We folded hands.
We bowed our heads.
We gave thanks for gifts.

We are still brothers.
We are family.
We are mature adults.

Now nearly 100 years old
Mother and father remain our rock,
Still talking and walking with God.

Characteristics

Tears
Sorrow
Suffering
Pain
Growth
Strength
Resilience

Love   → command or
                 characteristic?

The Black Woman

Claudia, Back Home

Recently,
a dachshund
with her short legs
left for the dog
motel
and the house hushed
and the neighbors missed
her constant barks—
and then the long trip
away from home made
her whine.
I don't know
whether dogs cry,
but I think this:
whoever leaves a dog
with strangers has
never considered the consequences—
how she gets quiet,
never sleeps,
when other dogs bark
all night long,
missing her owners—
counting the days when
they will return home
with unconditional love
shown from the time of adoption—
and how in the evening,
the other bitches wait
for their masters, but
this female jumps
into her master's arms,
assisting him
at the steering wheel
on their way home.

Elegy for Emmanuel

I remember his long legs, his dignified walk;
And his love for red and yellow roses,
And how, once beginning a conversation,
The jokes leaped at us,
And he laughed louder than everyone.
A happy soul, sensitive and kind.
Children sang and learned with him;
And friendly dogs looked up to him.
Oh, when he was sad, he sang "Precious
      Lord, Take My Hand."

The church members lifted him up with shouts:
Jumping over benches with a joyful noise;
All raising hands toward heaven.
My brother, you have gone,

Resting in Glory, saving room for us.
Visiting your grave cannot console me,
Nor the flowers surrounding your vault.
If only I could wake you from your sleep.

Grapes

I love eating red grapes all year
from the cold refrigerator, juicy
and seedless grapes for breakfast,
the color shining, the attention
they get for their beauty and
lusciousness, and as I savor them
one by one in my mouth, the rich
red grapes fall down my throat
with enjoyment, as words come to
me to describe the delicious experience:
succulent red grape eating, simply divine.

Today

today
   dogs
dash through
the snow
   into the yards of neighbors who protest.

today
the Bishop
leaves hundreds
   in the church split.

members clap
their hands
wipe tears
fall on their knees
heads bowed
whisper messages
   which are personal conferences with God.

today
I kiss my wife's lips
like my two dogs
kissing inside my house
and observe
through the window
our death-struggle
with Mother Nature.

today
my dogs
see me pray
again and again.

Deacon

He's still alive,

his 90 golden years
never slowing him
down—
        because he's lived right—

his nine children kept
him young
with their love
and good times
the church, too,
        there's no question
        that God kept him here—

Thanks to an 87-year-old queen
in his life for 67 years

He's eating her healthy food.

His Cadillac is always
ready to roll
        all over North Carolina

and, candidly speaking,
the Blind Boys
can't compete with his singing,

a deep bass voice
he praises God
        on his knees every Sunday
the songs from slavery
        still sung with the choir,

the Negro Spirituals
and Gospel pieces
the Call and Response
to the preacher's sermons,

and every week for 90 years
God held him in His bosom
and rocked him in the cradle
of His tender mercy.

The Vision of America

After such campaigns—what results?
What demarcation of votes? (to find
Among some regions rebelliousness that
Frightens freedom achieved based on merit.)

The Vision of America.
Model of rainbow coalitions:
Model of our desired equality:
Even the bloody history of our suffering.

We seek rights ancestors died for.
We seek Paradise here: flowers, sunlight,
Clouds, the rain for growth and harvest
In this new century of all colors.

We seek morning stars.
A triumph of noble spirit.
We see our gifts and our leader.
Redeemed America. And Obama.

The Geese

This morning
   the geese
      slept soundly
         by the pond

and opened their eyes—
   only when
      dental patients
         parked their cars,

feathers brown,
      their heads majestic
         with pride
            the pond mirroring them

and I uttered: poetry
      this is a subject for eternity,
         this is heaven's spot
            for life and love,

and the geese stood
      one flying into
         the pristine pond
            to swim slowly

enjoying the cool breeze
      helping it along
         and I opined: beauty,
            the dentist's office,

the pond, fish jumping,
      and that's when more geese
         flew into it
            for a celebration,

splashing freely
    and then cruising along the water—
        all the while quiet
            remaining together

indifferent to teeth pulled
    in the dentist's building
        or root canals
            and it seemed

they needed to fly away
    for new territory in the air, but
        the pond remained with all its glory
for all the world to savor.

God's Glory

Easter brought them to open country in North Carolina
Where they escaped various growing cities heavily populated.
Running in the fields where cotton and corn would later grow
Gave these angels freedom to explore the earth and sky.
Several stopped to pick purple clover flowers and dandelions;
Others kept following their uncle letting the soil tickle their feet.
They laughed with joy and excitement and admired airplanes
      roaring.
Four- and five-year-olds love blue jays and cardinals flying freely.
Children's songs of innocence can inspire parents and relatives
To cherish mental pictures frozen in time for wisdom and eternity.
Who says small angels cannot run and fly and take souls to God's
      Glory?

The Thought

Of resting forever in a mahogany coffin
And fighting off maggots from the body,
Sleeping without the aid of Tylenol PM,
Dressed up in a clean black suit
Red necktie and white shirt,
Hair slicked back with VO5,
Of owls hooting incessantly,
And buzzards hollering
Now that's what I call
Peace of mind and eternal happiness.

witty

Gratitude,
Spunky, turning
a depressing
situation into a lovely one — turning lemons into lemonade."

I Shall Pray

I shall keep praying!
Enemies will crucify me
On the job and in church,
Each—with nails for the cross.
I with humility
Will bleed profusely
With my hands stretched
And my head bowed.
I shall call His name;
I shall pray without ceasing.
Burial for my adversaries with earthworms
Will precede my own death.

Jesus

ACKNOWLEDGMENTS

Many thanks to the editors of the following magazines, in which some poems were previously published:

The Griot: Journal of the Southern Conference on African American Studies
Catalyst
The Zora Neale Hurston Forum
The Kentucky Poetry Review
The Black Scholar
Prophetic Voices: International Literary Journal
Testimony
Small Magazine
Essence Magazine
KOLA Magazine (Canada)
Classique

ABOUT THE AUTHOR

Leonard A. Slade Jr. received the bachelor's degree in English from North Carolina's Elizabeth City State University, the master's degree in English from Virginia State University, and the PhD degree in English from the University of Illinois at Urbana–Champaign. He taught for twenty-two years at Kentucky State University, where he was Chair of the Division of Literature, Languages, and Philosophy, and Dean of the College of Arts and Sciences. In May 1989, Kentucky State University awarded him the degree Doctor of Humane Letters. In May 1996, Elizabeth City State University awarded him a Doctor of Humane Letters degree. For several summers, he studied poetry at Bennington College, Vermont; at The Bread Loaf Writers' Conference, Middlebury College, Vermont; and at the Ragdale Artists' Colony, Lake Forest, Illinois. He studied with Pulitzer Prize winners Stephen Dunn and Donald Justice.

He has published in *Essence Magazine*, *U.S. News and World Report*, *The Courier-Journal*, *Ebony Magazine*, *The College Language Association Journal*, *The American Poetry Review*, *The Zora Neale Hurston Forum*, *The English Journal: Publication of the National Council of Teachers of English*, *The Journal of Southern History*, *The Black Scholar*, *The Kentucky Poetry Review*, *KOLA Magazine* (Canada), *Emerge Magazine*, *The Journal of Blacks in Higher Education*, *Catalyst*, *The ALAN Review: Publication of the National Council of Teachers of English*, *Little Magazine*, *The Griot: Journal of the Southern Conference on African American Studies*, and *Education Next: Journal of Opinion and Research* at Harvard University, to name a few. He has published eighteen books, including thirteen books of poetry: *Another Black Voice: A Different Drummer* (1988), *The Beauty of Blackness* (1989), *I Fly Like a Bird* (1992), *The Whipping Song* (1993), *Vintage* (1995), *Fire Burning* (1995), *Pure Light* (1996), *Neglecting the Flowers* (1997), *Lilacs in Spring* (1998), *Elisabeth and Other Poems* (1999), and *For the Love of Freedom* (2000). *Symbolism in Herman Melville's* Moby Dick:

From the Satanic to the Divine (1998) is his second book of literary criticism. *Jazz After Dinner*, his twelfth volume of poetry, was published by State University of New York Press in July 2006. He has read his poetry at Ohio State, Williams College, Skidmore College, Norfolk State, Virginia State, the universities of Missouri, Kentucky, Tennessee, Virginia, Arkansas, Illinois, Tufts, Duke, and Harvard, among others. His poetry has been praised by Maya Angelou, Gwendolyn Brooks, and Houston A. Baker, Jr.

Slade is former Chair and currently Professor of Africana Studies (Tenured), Adjunct Professor of English, and former Director of the Humanistic Studies Doctoral Program, and of the Master of Arts in Liberal Studies Program at State University of New York at Albany. In November 2007, he was named Citizens Academic Laureate at SUNY Albany. In April 2005, he was named a Collins Fellow at SUNY Albany. A past member of the National Research Center on the Teaching of Literature, he has been the recipient of the Excellence in Teaching Award at Kentucky State University and at State University of New York, Albany; the Professor of the Year Award from the SUNY NAACP chapter; the Kentucky Humanities Council Grant; the Hudson Mohawk Association of Colleges and Universities Award; the Northeast Modern Language Association Research Fellowship; the Ford Foundation Fellowship; the U.S. Department of State Fellowship for Postdoctoral Study; the Ragdale Artists' Fellowship, Lake Forest, Illinois; and the Recipient of the Southern Conference on African American Studies Book Awards. Under his leadership as Chair of the Department of Africana Studies, the Master's Program in Africana Studies was ranked number two in America three years in a row (2005, 2006, and 2007). He lives with his wife in Albany, New York.